LEGENDS OF NOT

By R. S. Holland

BRADWELL
BOOKS

Published by Bradwell Books

9 Orgreave Close Sheffield S13 9NP

Email: books@bradwellbooks.co.uk

British Library Cataloguing in Publication Data: a catalogue record for this book is available from the British Library.

1st Edition

ISBN: 9781909914971

Print: Berforts Information Press. Eynsham. OX29 4JB

Design by: Andrew Caffrey

Typesetting by: Mark Titterton

Photograph Credits: IStock and the author

Cover Photographs
Background image: Shutterstock/ Panos Karas
Green man image: Shutterstock/ Gwoeii
Robin Hood image: Shutterstock/ daseaford

CONTENTS

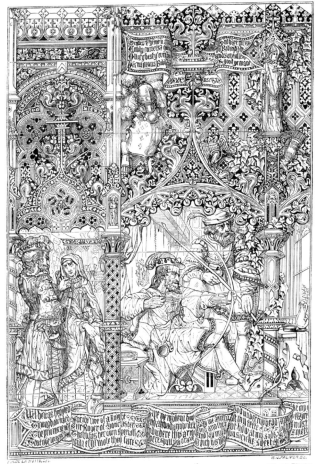

Robin Hood's last shot.

Nottinghamshire's most famous folk hero, Robin Hood, fires his final arrow.

INTRODUCTION

The folklore and folk tales of the British Isles make for an endlessly fascinating study. A glorious confusion of ancient beliefs has evolved over the millennia thanks to the many different races that have settled here. In England these have included Stone Age and Bonze Age tribes, the Iron Age Celts, then Romans, Angles, Saxons, Norsemen and Normans.

Into this cultural melting pot have been thrown any number of superstitions and half-remembered tales of cultural heroes, some real, some mythical, and many a mixture of both.

Our ancestors lived very different lives to those we enjoy today. Most were tied to the land and had an intimate relationship with the seasons and the natural world. Few had travelled further than their nearest market town, many had never even strayed that far from the rustic landscape they knew so well.

A 19th-century illustration depicting the verge of Sherwood Forest, a place central to much of Nottinghamshire's folklore.

The caves under Nottingham Castle have a sinister reputation and had an unexpected role to play in a medieval power struggle.

IStock Photo

Nevertheless, their seemingly limited existence was coloured with an awareness of another world, one where supernatural beings lived alongside them, just out of sight; where illness or death could be brought about not by microbes but by witchcraft; where familiar landmarks took on mystical significance. Heroes and villains from a past age lived again in dramatic legends told down the generations, while neighbouring communities were ridiculed by village wits, who invented tall tales about their idiocy and gullibility.

Robin Hood is, of course, Nottinghamshire's most famous folk hero and his legend has become well known throughout the world. There is a considerable heritage of folklore regarding the merry outlaw throughout the county. The evolution of his legend is fascinating to explore and one could take a very rewarding tour round all the places named after him.

However, there is far more to the lore of Nottinghamshire than just one man. This book is just a taster of the wealth of legends and superstitions which enlivened the imaginations of the county's rural residents a century or more ago.

The folklore of Nottinghamshire paints the county as a delightfully magical place. I hope you enjoy this brief tour through its wonders.

ROBIN HOOD AND HIS MERRY MEN

Almost everyone knows the legend of Robin Hood: a Saxon nobleman becomes an outlaw, retires to Sherwood Forest with a gang of merry men, and becomes a thorn in the side of the Sheriff of Nottingham, stealing his money and giving it to the poor. Such is the tale which has inspired countless movies and television series. In fact, such a straightforward narrative of Robin's adventures barely pre-dates the invention of the cinema. The legend of Robin Hood is certainly an old one but it is also obscure, fragmented and contradictory.

The oldest surviving literary work about Robin Hood's exploits is an anonymous ballad called *A Lytell Geste of Robyn Hode and his Meiny* (the last word meaning 'band'). This dates from the 15th century and is thought to have been based on four even older ballads. The first reference to the hero occurred a century earlier, however, in the 1377 version of William Langland's famous poem *The Vision of Piers Plowman*. In the poem a drunken man boasts that he can recite 'rymes of Robyn Hode'. Langland clearly expected his readers to recognise the name without further elucidation, showing that 'rymes' about Robin Hood had already become thoroughly established even longer ago.

Since those times, Robin Hood has grown to become Britain's best-known folk hero, arguably even more popular in terms of print, celluloid and video than his nearest rival, King Arthur. Like Arthur, there are sufficient stray historical references to imply that he may have been more than mythical, that there might be some kernel of truth behind the heroic tales. So who was he?

If he existed at all, it seems certain that he was from the North or the North Midlands. Most of the references in the early literature place him in Yorkshire, making his home in the Barnsdale Forest (only fragments of which now survive) and turning up in places such as Kirklees Abbey, near Leeds. There is a Robin Hood's Bay near Whitby, where tradition states the outlaw would keep boats for fishing or for making a quick escape.

Nevertheless, there are also a good many references to his activities in and around Sherwood Forest and of his being a scourge to the Sheriff of Nottingham. It's not inconceivable that a real outlaw might have been active over a wide area, or settled in different places at different times to avoid capture. In one part of the *Lytell Geste*, Robin is stated as being in Whitby with Little John. John has just joined the Merry Men and asks his leader who it's fair to steal from. Robin makes it clear that good, honest, hard-working people should be left in peace, but as an example of the sort of greedy gentry they should target, he states:

> 'The Hye Sheryfe of Notynghame,
> Hym hold in your minde.'

The modern narratives about Robin Hood set his activities during the reign of King John. John's high taxes and repressive regime are the spur for the outlaw's rebellion. One of the key motifs of many of these accounts is the unexpected return of King Richard from the Holy Land, in which he is presented as a saintly king, everything that John is not (although Richard's abandonment of his country and his subsequent capture by the French, who then

The popular image of Robin Hood as a romantic figure, bow in hand, ready to defend the oppressed.

issued a cripplingly high ransom demand, were largely responsible for the economic crisis).

In the *Lytell Geste*, however, the events are set during the reign of Edward II. Intriguingly, there is a historical reference to a 'Robyn Hode' who served as valet to Edward II during his stay at York in 1324. In this ballad, King Edward learns about the plundering carried out by outlaws in his royal forests and issues a proclamation that their leader should be apprehended and executed without delay. In disguise, the king carries out his own reconnaissance mission into the woods, only to be captured by the robbers. On discovering he has no money on him, the outlaws treat him kindly, much to the incognito king's surprise. The outlaws treat Edward to a meal of venison, which, of course, belongs to the king and should not have been hunted in the first place. Nevertheless, King Edward is much taken with Robin's personality and is pleased when the outlaw suddenly recognises him and immediately places himself and his band at the king's service, begging forgiveness for their infractions. Edward pardons them all and Robin joins the king's retinue.

This version of events appears to have inspired the later one regarding King Richard. He too is in disguise when he is captured by Robin's men in the greenwood. When Robin recognises the king, Richard pardons him and he helps his sovereign regain his throne. Edward II did journey north, in 1323, so it is tempting to wonder whether the Robyn Hode who was with him a year later really was an outlaw. But nothing in regards to Robin Hood is straightforward. Another source states that Robin was outlawed after taking part in a failed rebellion against Edward II by Thomas of Lancaster in 1322.

Confusing matters still further, a 16th-century chronicle insists that Robin was originally a supporter of Simon de Montfort, the powerful Earl of Leicester who led rebellious barons against Henry III in the 1260s. This Robin became an outlaw after de Montfort's defeat at the Battle of Evesham in 1265.

According to Jennifer Westwood and Jacqueline Simpson in their magnum opus of English folklore, *The Lore of the Land*, thirty-nine ballads and four short Elizabethan plays featuring Robin Hood are known to have been published between the late 15th century and the 18th. The details in most of them vary. Robin is not necessarily the dashing, Errol Flynn-type hero we imagine today. Robin Hood's habit of giving away his ill-gotten gains to the poor is a modern invention, for example. On the contrary, the old ballads made it quite clear that he kept the spoils for himself. Nevertheless, like other fictional bandits – Dick Turpin, for example – he could

Robin Hood encounters a fat bishop in this illustration from the 18th century. In all versions of the legend, Robin is an anti-establishment figure, waging war on greedy nobility and clergy.

be charming. The anonymous author of the *Lyttel Geste* comments that 'so curteyse an outlawe as he was one never non founde'. But only one ballad hints at any generosity toward the poor, and in just two lines:

> 'For he was a good outlaw
> And did poor men much good.'

It was Sir Walter Scott, better known as a keen collector and elaborator of folk tales from his native Scotland, who popularised the image of Robin Hood as freedom-fighting hero. In his novel *Ivanhoe*, published in 1820, Robin is introduced as a yeoman of solid stock ('Robert of Locksley') who has rebelled against Norman tyranny. He joins forces with the Saxon knight Ivanhoe to rescue his friends and to do King John another bad turn. A play published in 1601 has Robin as a displaced Saxon earl during the reign of Richard I, and Scott may have read this. At any rate, *Ivanhoe* cemented Robin's narrative as having taken place during the same period and established him as the brave, good-hearted outlaw we know today.

Jennifer Westwood and Jacqueline Simpson conclude: 'By the end of the 19th century, Robin typified light-hearted courage, cheeky defiance of tyranny, healthy country living, generosity, comradeship, and patriotism.'

Before we move on to some of his Nottinghamshire-based adventures, however, there is another element to the mythology of Robin Hood that we must consider. Some scholars have considered that, far from being a real historical character, Robin is in fact a medieval reimagining of ancient pagan beliefs. Traditions regarding fairies, so common in other parts of England, appear to be lacking in Nottinghamshire, but they might in fact survive as the forest-dwelling Merry Men. As creatures of the wild places, fairies were traditionally believed to dress in green, and the Merry Men were famous for wearing Lincoln green. They were mischievous characters who lived in the depths of the woods, just like fairies.

The name 'Robin' has a history in pre-Christian tradition. Robin Goodfellow was a fun-loving sprite said to be the offspring of the King of the Fairies and a mortal woman, and the name is used by Shakespeare's Puck in *A Midsummer Night's Dream*. 'Robin' also has links to an archaic word 'hob', which refers to a devil (as in 'hobgoblin').

In the early Middle Ages, Nottinghamshire was for many years part of the Danelaw, under the control of Norse settlers. Naturally, these Norsemen brought their beliefs with them and Robin Hood has also been associated with one of their gods, Hod or Hoder. Hoder was a bowman, like Robin, who was tricked by the wicked Loki into firing an arrow at the most favoured of the gods, Baldur. Robin's habit of donning disguises and of defeating his foes through wit rather than by force also links him to certain kinds of fairy tales and ancient traditions of 'trickster gods'.

It has also been suggested that Robin Hood and his beloved Maid Marian were late survivors of a tradition of male and female fertility gods. They were popular characters at May Day and Midsummer celebrations, with a boy and a girl acting out both roles, in what were often sanitised versions of pagan customs. There is certainly something otherworldly about Robin and his men; living in seclusion in the greenwood, entering and leaving the civilised world at will, causing mayhem with impunity before vanishing away again from mortal eyes.

The bronze statue of Robin Hood which greets visitors to Nottingham Castle. Robin Hood's popularity has remained undiminished century after century.

IStock Photo

ROBIN OF SHERWOOD

When the Domesday Book was compiled in 1086, Sherwood Forest covered as much as a quarter of Nottinghamshire. It also extended into neighbouring counties. Today there is just over a thousand acres left. Originally 'forest' meant an area of country set aside for hunting and would include heath as well as woodland. Sherwood (meaning 'the shire wood') was a Royal Forest set aside for the pleasure of the king and his courtiers. The deer, in particular, were protected under law and could not be killed by anyone without the royal seal of approval. Those who broke this law could find themselves at the end of a rope.

Robin Hood and his Merry Men, of course, took no notice of such rules and regulations. As we have heard, there are a number of references placing England's most famous outlaws in Sherwood Forest and a good many local traditions highlighting his supposed activities in the region. In these tales his arch-enemy is the cruel and oppressive Sheriff of Nottingham. The folklorist Christina Hole relates a centuries-old story relating to a desperate fight Robin had in Nottingham. She writes:

'Once when Robin went alone to St Mary's Church in Nottingham, a monk in the congregation recognised him, and ran out to raise the alarm. The sheriff and a great crowd of townsmen came pouring into the church to take the outlaw. He was still kneeling in prayer, unaware of the danger, when they arrived, but he managed to kill twelve of them with his sword before he was taken prisoner. 'Little John and Much the Miller's son rescued him soon afterwards but not before they had taken revenge on the betrayer of their master. The monk was sent to Nottingham to inform the king of Robin's capture, and when, on his way, he encountered two young men whom he took to be respectable yeomen, he was foolish enough to boast of his part in the affair. The two outlaws murdered him on the spot.'

Robin Hood and Little John enjoy a chortle while wandering through Sherwood Forest. This Victorian illustration by N.C. Wyeth perfectly captures the jovial character of the sanitised Robin Hood legends, which had little to do with their medieval originals.

Such a brutal story hardly equates with the character of jovial champion of the poor that Robin has now acquired. Murdering monks and slaughtering townspeople in a church are two scenes one wouldn't expect in an Errol Flynn movie. Nevertheless, Robin is still portrayed as a hero because of the baseness of the act of attacking him while he is at his devotions. This is a shocking transgression of the sanctity of the church on behalf of the sheriff.

There are many other stories regarding the outlaws' scraps with the Sheriff of Nottingham. The villain's stronghold, Nottingham Castle, has become almost as well known as Robin Hood himself. These ripping yarns are largely 19th-century elaborations of incidents set down in 17th- or 18th-century plays and poems.

In one well-worn adventure, Robin takes part in an archery contest at Nottingham Castle, heavily disguised. He wins the prize of a golden arrow and catches the attention of Maid Marian for the first time. In another, he dons the apparel of an old man to gain access to the castle as part of a plan to rescue the three sons of a poor widow who are to be hanged for poaching. Robin requests the 'honour' of being hangman, but instead cuts free the prisoners and, with a blast of his hunting horn, summons his Merry Men. They fight their way out of the castle and escape to the greenwood.

A third adventure sees Robin Hood, this time disguised as a butcher, calling at the castle in order to find out what has happened to his right-hand man, Little John. It turns out that John has reluctantly entered the Sheriff of Nottingham's service, having made himself too prominent during the annual fair. Unaware of his true identity, the sheriff hires him after he wins both the wrestling and the archery contests. Little John finds himself in an impossible situation but takes comfort by fighting the other servants and consuming large quantities of the sheriff's food and

The massive gateway into Nottingham Castle, the stronghold of Robin Hood's arch-enemy, the sheriff.

IStock Photo

wine. In the belief that Robin is a butcher with a herd of cattle to sell at a bargain price, the sheriff is tricked into travelling into Sherwood Forest. Little John accompanies them. The sheriff soon finds himself at the mercy of the Merry Men, and Little John is released from his service.

A gentler tradition is attached to the village of Edwinstowe, which is situated at the heart of what remains of Sherwood Forest. At the entrance to the churchyard there is a little plaque informing visitors that it is here that Robin Hood and Maid Marian got married. If the couple ever existed, this is not impossible, for the current church dates back to the 12th century and a 6th-century church originally stood on the site. Another, equally vague tradition says that one of the Merry Men, the minstrel Alan-a-Dale, was married to his ladylove in the church at Papplewick.

According to tradition, on their deaths Robin and most of his cohorts were laid to rest in a number of locations in Yorkshire. A memorial in the churchyard at Blidworth, however, was long pointed out as marking the burial place of Will Scarlet. A marble plaque forming part of the memorial shows a lively hunting scene, including a stag and hounds and men with longbows. Despite the fact that the stone is clearly commemorating a man named Leake, this image has been enough to create a connection with the Robin Hood legend. Why Will Scarlet, rather than any of the other Merry Men, should have been chosen for this honour is anyone's guess.

In contrast to this dubious connection, Westwood and Simpson can point to a skirmish involving real medieval outlaws at Blidworth. In 1276, the steward of Sherwood Forest, John de Lascelles (what a Norman name that is!), apprehended two men in the woods armed with bows and arrows. The carrying of a bow in the forest was illegal because it could only mean one thing: that they were after the king's deer. The steward brought the men out of Sherwood to Blidworth, where he lived. He then imprisoned them in a neighbouring house (why not his own is not recorded). Presumably, de Lascelles' intention was to take them to Nottingham for trial the next day. That night, however, a gang of at least twenty armed men raided the house where they were being held, overpowered the guards and set them free. They all then went to the steward's house. Unable to gain entrance, they broke his windows and shouted abuse before vanishing back into the forest.

One of the most memorable encounters recorded in the annals of Robin Hood is the hero's meeting with Friar Tuck. Greedy monks and other members of the clergy were an established figure of satire in the Middle Ages, and their guzzling caricatures can be found in church decorations all over the country. Robin Hood was a particular scourge of those running monastic institutions who spent their great wealth on their own bodily comforts rather than those of the poor. 'Tuck' is another word for food, as in 'tuck in' and 'tuck shop', which would square with the good friar's reputation for portliness.

When Robin spied the fat friar feeding his face under a tree beside a stream in Sherwood Forest, he marked him out at once as his lawful prey. Drawing his sword, he forced Tuck to give him a piggyback across the stream. However, the plump monk was not the slouch he appeared to be, and after they had reached the opposite bank, he succeeded in turning the tables on Robin and forced the surprised outlaw to carry him back. Robin realised he had met with an extraordinary personality and invited Friar Tuck to see to the spiritual well-being of the Merry Men.

This story appears in two old ballads, *Robine Hood and Ffryer Tucke* and *The Famous Battel Between Robin Hood and the Curtal Friar*. 'Curtal'

Edwinstowe Church, where Robin Hood and Maid Marian are popularly believed to have been married.

apparently means short-robed. According to Nottinghamshire tradition, the scene of this adventure is Fountain Dale, near Blidworth. The stream in the story is the River Rain.

Several places around Fountain Dale continued to have an association with Friar Tuck until the 19th century. They included 'Friar Tuck's Cell', a tiny building unfortunately destroyed by a farmer who decided to find a use for its stone. There were also two water sources called 'Friar Tuck's Well' near Fountain Dale. One of them was a chalybeate spring (containing iron salts) which was believed to have medicinal properties. It was sufficiently important at one time to have had a wall built around it and to be topped off with a stone well head. Today both these structures are in ruins.

While we're on the subject of wells, artefacts allegedly belonging to the great outlaw were formerly on show at a little museum attached to Robin Hood's Well in Nottingham (see the 'Sacred Springs' chapter). Rather pathetically, by the close of the 18th century only two exhibits remained: a cap or helmet Robin was said to have worn and 'a part of his chair' (not even the entire chair!).

There is no shortage of remembrances of Robin around what remains of Sherwood Forest. Near Newstead Abbey, for example, we find Robin Hood's Hills, among which can also be found Robin Hood's Cave and Robin Hood's Chair. The latter, needless to say, is not the same fragment of furniture formerly kept at Robin Hood's Well in Nottingham, but an outcrop of rock from which the outlaw was supposed to survey the countryside. The cave was credited as being one of his hideouts.

Friar Tuck is forced to carry a certain notorious outlaw across a stream. This amusing encounter between Robin Hood and Friar Tuck is said to have taken place at Fountain Dale.

The Major Oak in Sherwood Forest, where Robin Hood and his Merry Men would meet and sleep.

iStock Photo

Elsewhere in the UK, notable landmarks were said to have been made by giants or the Devil. In Nottinghamshire they are invariably linked to Robin Hood, showing his supremacy as a folk hero in this part of the country.

There is another Robin Hood's Cave in the parish of Waulby and another Robin Hood's Hill near Oxton. The latter is a prehistoric burial mound. Despite the fact that there is no local tradition regarding Robin's death (usually said to have taken place at Kirklees Abbey in Yorkshire), a number of places called Robin Hood's Grave were marked on old maps of Nottinghamshire. There were also at least two Robin Hood's Farms. At Papplewick Hall a rough chamber carved out of a sandstone outcrop in the grounds was known as Robin Hood's Stable. Its use as a stable was recorded long ago but the link with Robin appears to have been a Victorian invention.

In addition, several of Sherwood's great trees featured in the folklore of the merry outlaws. The Parliament Oak at Clipstone is one of those under which Robin was said to have plotted his daring schemes with his men. The Parliament Oak is a slim shadow of its former self. At one time it was an impressive 25 feet (8 metres) in diameter. What survives today is the growth from one of its offshoots. Both Edward I and John I are credited with holding impromptu parliaments under the tree at times of crisis, hence its name. Perhaps Robin referred to his meetings as parliaments, too, in a spirit of fun.

The Major Oak is the other tree pointed out as one of Robin Hood's rendezvous sites. This is Sherwood Forest's most famous tree, an amazing survivor, perhaps up to a thousand years old, with a girth measuring more than 30 feet (10 metres). Its largest limbs are now propped up to prevent them falling and damaging the trunk. So mighty is the Major Oak, it was said the Merry Men used to sleep in its canopy. Of course, it would have been little more than a sapling in Robin's time, but folklore has no use for logic.

It's perfectly reasonable to suppose that prominent trees in the forest would have proved useful rallying places for real outlaws as well as legendary ones. Dim recollections of the activities of the many poachers and other outlaws active in Sherwood Forest at one time may well have been appropriated to the growing legend of Robin Hood. This certainly seems to have been the case with another majestic old oak, formerly growing near Ollerton. It went by many names over the years, including Slaughter Tree, Butcher's Tree, Shambles (i.e. a butcher's shop) and Hooton's Oak.

This last name is the original one, or so implies Pat Mayfield in *Legends of Nottinghamshire*. Hooton was a notorious poacher and sheep rustler, who would cut up the carcases of the stolen animals and hang them on hooks around the great hollow space within the tree. Later on, Hooton's cunning ruse was transplanted to Robin Hood. It was he, more recent tourist guides asserted, who lined the tree's interior with hooks and he who hung upon them joints of venison from the king's deer. So in time the tree (which finally collapsed in the 1950s) stopped being called Hooton's Oak and became instead Robin Hood's Larder.

THE UNEXPECTED GUEST

Robin Hood is not the only notable figure to feature in legends of Sherwood Forest. An old ballad tells a jolly tale of a royal guest who foists himself on a miller in Mansfield. Mansfield was sometimes used as a base by royal parties intending to enjoy some sport in Sherwood. One day, one of the King Henries became separated from his cronies and got lost in the forest. One version of the ballad names Henry II as the protagonist but the most popular makes it Henry VIII. The Tudor king is a more colourful character and one known to be addicted to the chase.

In the story, King Henry wanders round Sherwood Forest for some hours, he and his horse becoming more and more exhausted and bedraggled. Finally, somebody comes into view and the king approaches him with relief. But he is met with anything but open arms. His 'rescuer' is John Cockle, the Mansfield miller. A shrewd man, John Cockle doesn't like the look of this burly character in grubby finery. He assumes he's a 'gentleman robber' and tells him to be on his guard. Surprised but amused by this reception, the king does his best to reassure the pugnacious miller but decides not to reveal his true identity. Instead, he pretends to be merely a traveller who has lost his way.

Mollified, the miller invites the stranger home but gruffly warns him not to expect luxury. There'll be plain but wholesome food, rough but clean sheets and he'll have to share a bed with his son. Back at the mill, Cockle helps the king wipe down his horse and stable it with fresh straw. Then they sit down to supper. Henry tucks into some of the most delicious pasties he has ever eaten. But there's a problem. They are made of venison. And hunting the deer of Sherwood Forest is forbidden. Henry praises the miller's wife's cooking but enquires about their contents. The guileless miller's son admits that they enjoy venison every day, but begs their guest to keep that to himself, for the penalty for poaching the king's deer is death.

The king keeps his counsel and finds himself more and more enjoying his unconventional evening. Completely unaware that he is entertaining his sovereign, John Cockle cheerfully puts the world to rights with his appreciative guest.

The following morning, after an early breakfast, Cockle shows his new friend the right road back to town. Henry is saying his goodbyes when a party of courtiers, out looking for the missing king, ride into view. As soon as they recognise him, they jump from their horses and kneel before their monarch. John Cockle immediately sees his danger. In a flash, he recalls the venison pasties and his free talk. He falls to his knees, expecting nothing more than to be seized and dragged off to the gallows.

King Henry is a much more generous master than that, however. Not only is he grateful for John's hospitality, but he found the experience of not being a king for a day a liberating and educational one. He draws his sword. The miller closes his eyes and holds his breath. The king touches him lightly on both shoulders and knights him! The royal party ride away, His Majesty chuckling merrily, leaving behind a bemused Sir John Cockle trying to get used to his new nobility.

Later, the king puts Sir John's status on a surer footing. With the idea of setting a thief to catch a thief, he makes the miller overseer of Sherwood Forest and provides him with a pension of £300 a year. There is just one stipulation – he must never poach the king's deer again.

King Henry VIII got a surprise when he stayed with a miller in Mansfield, but not as great as the one the miller got when he learned the identity of his guest.

THE WISE MEN OF GOTHAM

Once upon a time it wasn't uncommon for rivalry to exist between villages in the English countryside. This antipathy would manifest most strongly at sporting events and fairs, all too often with a punch-up. A more imaginative and less traumatic way to express scorn for a neighbouring community, however, was to tell jokes about them. Stories illustrating their stupidity were particularly popular. For some reason, in Nottinghamshire the targeted village for such japery was Gotham. Take, for example, the well-known ditty:

'Three wise men of Gotham
Went to sea in a bowl;
And if the bowl had been stronger,
My song would have been longer.'

By the 17th century there was a recognised saying, 'As wise as a wise man of Gotham', meaning, in fact, a fool. One yarn about the 'foles of Gotham' dates back to the 15th century:

Two farmers on their way to market meet on a bridge. They greet each other and discover that each is intending to buy a flock of sheep. Asks one: 'How will you bring them back to Gotham?' 'Why, over this bridge,' replies the other. 'Nay, but thou shalt not!' insists his rival. 'By God, but I will!' counters the other. So incensed are they at the idea of two flocks of sheep – neither of which they have yet purchased – trying to cross the same narrow bridge that they come to blows. A miller now comes upon the scene. When he learns what the two farmers are fighting about, he upturns a sack of meal over the parapet of the bridge into the river below. When all the meal has poured away, the miller tells the squabbling men that their heads are as empty as his sack.

Gothamite millers weren't immune from leg-pulling, however. An anecdote recalls the miller who was worried about weighing down his horse with two heavy sacks of wheat. To save it from the strain, he hoisted one of them onto his own back — but then climbed on the horse. Then there is the Gotham smith who, in order to smoke out a few wasps, burned down his smithy, or the Gotham bridegroom who said 'After me' every time the priest used the phrase 'Say after me…'

Hardly side-splitting stuff by today's standards but they were thought sufficiently amusing to be collected together into a book as long ago as 1565, when *Merie Tales of the Mad Men of Gotam* was published.

According to an account published two centuries later, the reputation for idiocy was fostered by the villagers of Gotham themselves. They did so to escape punishment from Bad King John. The Gothamites got wind of the fact that the king was on his way to Nottingham and had chosen a route through their fields. Aware that any route taken by a king immediately becomes a public highway, they came up with various ways of preventing him from doing so. The king ended up bypassing Gotham, but not before coming to the conclusion that his way had been deliberately blocked. He later sent officers of the Crown to Gotham so that they could investigate the matter and determine the most effective means of punishment.

The people of Gotham went to great lengths to prove they were idiots. One of their foolish escapades involved them trying to hedge in a cuckoo.

Fortunately, the Gothamites got word of this royal visitation. They decided that if they could convince the officers they were complete simpletons, not responsible for their own actions, this might 'turn away His Majesty's displeasure from them'.

When the officers arrived, they found the villagers engaged in a roster of ridiculous tasks. These included trying to drown an eel in a pond; tumbling cheeses down a hill in the belief they would find their own way to Nottingham market; and hedging in a bush on which a cuckoo was sitting in order to trap it. Behind this last foolishness was the idea that because the cuckoo is a harbinger of summer, trapping it would mean having summer all year long. If this wasn't stupid enough, they'd apparently forgotten that the cuckoo could fly away, which it did. The hedging in of the cuckoo is still recorded in a local place name, Cuckoo Bush Farm. The emissaries returned to the king convinced Gotham was a village of buffoons and not worth bothering with.

MORE NOTABLE CHARACTERS AND EVENTS

The Goose Fair has been an annual event in Nottingham since the 13th century. Held in October, the fair was an opportunity for traders from outside the area, including foreigners, to sell their wares to the people of Nottingham. Its odd name was first recorded in 1541. The most straightforward reason for it is that the fair started off as one exclusively set aside for the selling of geese at Michaelmastide. To eat a goose on Old Michaelmas Day (11 October) was considered very lucky in Nottinghamshire, as an old rhyme testifies:

> 'He who eats goose on Michaelmas Day,
> Shan't money lack his debts to pay.'

Geese certainly remained among the livestock sold at the Goose Fair, for they were driven up from Lincolnshire, Norfolk and elsewhere to take advantage of this superstition. This proved far too simple an explanation for the storytellers of the past, however. Two preposterous yarns have been reeled out offering alternative explanations for the Goose Fair's origin.

One is that an angler was fishing one day in the River Trent when he was lucky enough to catch a big pike. He was yanking the fish out of the river when an enormous goose swooped down and grabbed it. The bird flew off with the pike, taking the unfortunate angler with it as well. Not surprisingly, the goose was unable to hold onto this heavy cargo for long. While flying over Nottingham, it opened its beak and both man and pike plummeted into the Market Place. The angler survived his fall remarkably unscathed (the story does not record the state of the fish) and the townsfolk celebrated his deliverance with a holiday.

Even sillier is the tale of a young bumpkin who was brought up on an isolated farm by his father. The boy's mother had died many years ago. He lived such a sheltered life with his father that he had never met a woman. The first time he saw girls was on his first ever trip to Nottingham Goose Fair.

'Father, what are these strange creatures?' he asked.

His embarrassed father became flustered and replied: 'Geese.'

This comment was overheard and the marketers were highly entertained by the youngster's first introduction to the 'geese' of their city. The event became informally known as the Goose Fair from then on.

Bearing in mind the above tale, it is sobering to recall that women were once among the commodities sold at Nottingham Goose Fair. Long ago it was legal to auction off a wife. This barbaric custom was made even more humiliating by each unhappy woman being forced to wear a horse's collar during the auction. But the riot that took place at the Goose Fair in the 1760s was down to a much humbler product: cheese. As Polly Howat explains in her *Tales of Old Nottinghamshire*, the local farmers made a pact to increase the price of their cheese by about a third. When the people saw the new inflated prices they were incensed and were not subtle about showing their displeasure.

Cheesemongers were attacked, their stalls overthrown and their produce stolen. When the mayor stood up to call for calm, someone threw a whole cheese at him and he was knocked unconscious. This was the cue for an unusually violent food fight, with heavy rounds of cheese hurled at farmers and the militia. Dragoons from Nottingham Castle fired into the crowd but only succeeded in killing a cheesemonger named William Egglestone who was desperately trying to guard his stall. This bizarre incident has become known as the Great Cheese Riot.

Riots also broke out the following century when 'framemakers' working for hosiers in Nottingham and elsewhere petitioned for a living wage. In the early 1800s the manufacture of silk socks and stockings was one of the county's most important industries, but those actually doing the work of making them were paid a pittance.

IStock Photo

A sheltered youth mistook girls for geese in Nottingham, his extraordinary blunder supposedly inspiring the name of its annual fair.

A series of violent disturbances broke out when Nottingham factory owners refused to meet their employees' and subcontractors' demands for better pay. In time the campaign of violence against employers and their property became more organised. In 1811 bills and petitions by the agitators were undersigned by their supposed leader, one 'Ned Ludd'.

Lud is the name of a mythical ancient king who supposedly founded London. Ludgate is named after him. A prehistoric earthwork in neighbouring Leicestershire is known as 'King Lud's Entrenchments'. Lud is probably the name of a Celtic deity. It is unknown where the Luddites, as they came to be known, found the name Ned Ludd, but a story developed to give him an identity. He was supposedly a simpleton from a Nottinghamshire village who was constantly being picked on by the local kids. Ned would endure the teasing for as long as he could, but eventually his frustration would boil over and he'd lose his temper. On one occasion he took his rage out on a couple of knitting frames, smashing them to pieces. From then on, says the tradition, Ned Ludd became a scapegoat for such outrages and that is why his name was adopted by the smashers of machinery.

Nottinghamshire has had more than its fair share of eccentrics over the years. One of these was undoubtedly Sir Thomas Parkyns, the 'Wrestling Baronet'. Sir Thomas was squire of Bunny Hall during the first half of the 18th century. He took his duties seriously, improving the estates round Bunny and Bradmore, building almshouses and a school. He was keen on architecture and designed many of the buildings he commissioned, including a distinctive wall round Bunny Hall. He was an intelligent and learned man but there was one thing Sir Thomas Parkyns loved above all else: wrestling.

An engraving of Sir Thomas Parkyns, the Wrestling Baronet, in typical pose.

Sir Thomas was addicted to wrestling. He wrote a book called *The Cornish Hug Wrestler* and inaugurated an annual wrestling match in Bunny village in 1712. This proved extremely popular. It was open to all and the prize was a gold-laced hat. The Wrestling Baronet would compete, too, along with a number of his male servants. All considerations of class were literally thrown aside during the match. There can't have been many footmen in England who got the chance to hurl their master flat on his back and get praised for it.

Unfortunately, as is so often the case, the event attracted the wrong sort; and far too many of them. Idlers would take the opportunity to get drunk and obnoxious and petty thieves would have a field day. So riotous did the Bunny Wrestling Match become that it was finally suppressed in 1811. By this time Sir Thomas was long dead. He had died in 1741, at the age of 78. His rather splendid memorial in Bunny Church shows him in wrestling pose.

Another eccentric individual, the Earl of Oxford, is said to have taken part in an impressive, if rather foolish, feat at his stately home, Welbeck Abbey. A huge tree, called the Greendale Oak, formerly stood in Welbeck Abbey's grounds. It was so tall and so wide that one day the Earl reckoned a hole could be made in it sufficient for a carriage-and-pair to be driven through. A visiting guest challenged him to prove the assertion and it became a wager between them.

The Earl gave the order to his workmen, and a vast arch was dug out of the Greendale Oak's trunk. Sure enough, a coach pulled by two horses was driven safely through the arch and the Earl won his bet. The wood that had been removed was made into a writing desk for his wife, the Countess of Oxford. Sadly, this gross vandalism was too much for the tree and a few years later it died. Nothing remains of it today.

SACRED SPRINGS

Nottinghamshire is blessed with a large number of wells and springs, each with an interesting tradition belonging to it. Many were believed to have medicinal properties. One of the most famous of these was St Ann's Well in Nottingham. In the 14th century it was recorded as being called 'Robynhode Well', another link to the famous outlaw. When a chapel dedicated to St Anne was built nearby a century later, the well was renamed in her honour (the saint's name is usually spelled with an 'e' these days). However, the townsfolk continued to call it Robin Hood's Well.

After the Dissolution of the Monasteries, St Ann's Chapel and Well came to be used as a health resort. The waters were said to cure either one of two highly disparate ailments, rheumatism or impotence. It's not easy to see how the water could improve one's sexual prowess or aid rheumatism, for by all accounts it was extremely cold. One visitor in the 18th century described it as being so cold, 'it will kill a toad'. St Ann's Well was buried under a railway embankment in 1887 but was recently excavated and found to still be flowing, through an underground culvert.

Just as celebrated in its day was St Catherine's Well, on the outskirts of Newark-on-Trent. Its waters were reputed to cure leprosy, that grim scourge of the Middle Ages. A legend exists to explain the origin of the well and its curative properties. It is a romantic yarn of crossed love, murder and redemption, just the sort of heady stuff beloved by 19th-century antiquarians.

According to the story, two noble knights, Sir Guy Saucimer and Sir Everard Bevercotes, were fast friends, but unfortunately they fell in love with the same girl. The object of their affection was Isabell, the beautiful daughter of a man with the suspiciously suitable name of Alan de Caldwell ('cold well'). Isabell was fond of both her suitors but, of course, could only choose one. She gave her hand to Sir Everard. Learning of their betrothal, Sir Guy went mad with grief. He fought Sir Everard, whom he accused of betraying their friendship, and killed him. The date of this tragedy was 24 November, St Catherine's Day. Where Sir Everard's body fell, a spring of clear, pure water burst out of the ground.

Horrified by what he'd done, Sir Guy exiled himself abroad. He wandered, a morose outcast, for a number of years, some say to the Holy Land. In his wanderings had the misfortune to contract leprosy. At about the same time word reached him that Isabell had died of a broken heart. He decided to make his way back to Nottinghamshire to try to make amends for his terrible deed before he died. It was a long, slow journey. At length he reached France where, one night, while sleeping in the forest of St Avold, on the German border, he was visited in a dream by St Catherine. The saint told him that his leprosy could be cured by the water which had sprung up where Sir Everard fell.

With renewed purpose, Sir Guy returned to Newark and used the water from the spring to rid himself of his disease. Then he built for himself a rough cell beside the River Devon, into which the spring water ran, and planned a life of impoverished contemplation. He wasn't there long, though, before the river overflowed and forced him to move to a drier spot. Here he built a slightly more elaborate hermitage, with a chapel attached. In the chapel he sculpted the scene of Sir Everard Bevercotes' death and the miraculous creation of the spring, together with a figure of St

Catherine. He also walled in and tended the sacred spring. Here Sir Guy lived all the rest of his life, a wise and humble holy man who in time became known as St Guthred.

And that's the story of St Catherine's Well. No historical source exists for it, however, and it is quite possibly fictional. It was originally set down in a book about Newark published in 1819, but at least one modern scholar believes it was a hoax foisted on the unwitting author.

The attractive structure surrounding St Ann's Well in Nottingham, photographed before it was buried under a railway embankment. (Picture of the Past)

A similarly romantic tale involving noble knights used to be told about Willow Rundle Spring, another medicinal water source near the village of Elston. In *A History of Nottinghamshire*, published in 1891, Cornelius Brown writes: 'A soldier fell in the battle, and a comrade came to his assistance, and gave him water from his bottle. Feeling he was dying, he told his friend that if his soul went to paradise, there would arise from the spot where he fell a spring that would flow on forever.'

The battle concerned is the Battle of Stoke Field, which is considered the last big scrap of the War of the Roses. It involved more men and horses and even bloodier fighting than the much better known Battle of Bosworth in neighbouring Leicestershire. The war was effectively over when the battle at East Stoke was fought in July 1487, for Henry Tudor had taken the throne from Richard III two years previously. The Battle of Stoke Field was fought between the forces of the newly crowned Henry VII and Yorkists who refused to accept the legitimacy of his reign and hoped to place a usurper with a doubtful pedigree on the throne instead. By losing this battle, the House of York lost any further chance of gaining control of the throne of England.

A macabre tradition related to Willow Rundle Spring is that the hearts of the Yorkists were staked into the ground with staves of willow and buried there to rot. This brutal ritual may have been carried out because it was feared that the slain would return as ghosts. The spirits of people who had died a sudden death were formerly believed to be at risk of wandering the earth, especially if their bodies had not been buried in consecrated ground. Until the 19th century, suicides were denied burial in churchyards and were often interred in lonely spots with stakes through their hearts. Today the belief lingers in popular film and literature as the best means to dispatch a vampire. Henry VII had all the clergymen who had supported the Yorkists' campaign excommunicated, so it's not unreasonable to suppose that he was vengeful enough to deny his enemies the dignity of a proper burial.

A much more pleasant tradition, as recorded by Cornelius Brown, is that the spring 'has never been known to dry up in the hottest summer, or to be frozen over in the coldest winter'. In Brown's day the spring poured into a 'modern' trough, the worn remains of which survive to this day.

WITCHES AND THE DARK ARTS

For many centuries, it was believed that misfortune, illness and even death could be willed upon a person by another skilled in mystic arts or who had been given the power to do so by the Devil. Because witchcraft appears in the Bible (for example, in the story of the Witch of Endor and the conjuring up of a demon for King Solomon), the dark arts were believed in as firmly by educated people as the illiterate.

It might seem the height of foolish ignorance to believe in witchcraft but it should be remembered that prior to the 18th century almost nothing was understood about the causes of disease. Microbes were unknown. We believe in the virus giving us a cold even though we have never seen it, and our ancestors believed in the existence of witchcraft with the same degree of certainty.

So firm was the belief in witchcraft that someone accused of cursing an animal or human to fall ill or die was treated just the same as if they had poisoned or murdered their victims by more orthodox means. The criminal justice system saw no difference: the end result was all that mattered. By the dawn of the 17th century, however, Europe had fallen into the grip of a 'witch mania', fuelled in part by the resurgence of bubonic plague and by religious insecurity fanned by the Renaissance. No one was safe from being accused of being a witch. Lonely old women, especially those who had previously been known to provide herbal remedies, harmless love charms and the like, were early targets, but even the nobility found themselves accused, often by the unscrupulous as a means of getting them out of the way. Thousands of supposed witches and male sorcerers were hanged or burned alive as the mania swept Europe.

Nottinghamshire appears to have escaped the worst of the panic, with most of its trials for witchcraft being conducted in the late 16th century and the first few decades of the 17th. In their excellent book *Witch-Hunting in England*, authors Andrew and David Pickering have compiled a – mercifully short – list of women indicted for witchcraft in Nottinghamshire, with the dates of their indictments: Margaret Frore, of Harby, 1606; Isabella Cotton, of Hayton, 1608; Joan Clark, of Sutton in the Clay, 1609; Barbara Daste, of Broughton Sulney, 1609; Christian Clark and two women named Hudson, 1616; Helen Beckett, of West Drayton, 1621; Alice Busse, of Bagthorpe, and an unnamed woman of Boughton, 1623; Katherine Brown, of Cromwell, 1629. In addition, there is an extraordinary case involving John Darrell and William Somers, more of which in the next chapter.

Naturally, with such a strong belief in malevolent witches being present, stories about their supposed activity passed into folklore. A legend about a shape-shifting witch, of a type common in the UK, is told about Sutton-on-Trent. This witch had a grudge against the wife of a weaver. When the woman was lying sick in bed – the illness brought about perhaps by the dark arts – her chamber was invaded by 'an ugly great cat'. The cat had been spotted by her children, creeping up the stairs, but when they tried to grab it, it kept dodging out of their way. It slinked into their mother's room and leapt on her bed, striking out at her with its claws. The weaver's wife managed to defend herself and knocked the cat to the floor, and it ran off.

When the weaver got home from selling cloth at Newark market, his wife and frightened children told him about the cat's attack. He had a good look round the house and found a broken window-pane in the lumber room, through which, he guessed, the animal had come and gone. He watched all night and the next to see if it would return. Sure enough, he saw the cat squeezing in through the gap in the window. Grabbing a hay-fork, he leapt up and stabbed the cat in the cheek. It fell to the floor, apparently dead, and he threw the carcase outside. The following morning, the carcase had vanished. But they were never bothered by the cat again. When the old witch was next seen, her face was tied up with a bloody bandage and she had lost all her power.

In *Legends of Nottinghamshire*, Pat Mayfield recounts a legend about a witch near Rempstone (another possible location for the story is

IStock Photo

An old engraving of witches' revels. Images like these propagated the fear of witchcraft throughout the 16th and 17th centuries.

Retford). This hag used the fear of her powers to extort food from her neighbours. One day she begged at a lowly shack inhabited by an elderly widow and her son, Jack. She saw they had a pail of buttermilk and instantly demanded it. But the buttermilk was Jack and his mother's only source of income. Generous neighbours would allow Jack to take it away after churning their butter and he would sell it to farmers for animal feed. If he gave it away to the witch, they would starve. He refused.

The witch was furious. She was not accustomed to refusals. She demanded the buttermilk again, saying that if he didn't comply she would put him in her sack and take him away instead. Jack laughed at this and told her to go about her business. The next moment, to his astonishment, he found himself tumbled into the witch's sack and carted away.

On her way back to her cottage, the hag suddenly remembered she'd left a pot of lard back in Rempstone. She left the sack with two men cutting the hedge by the side of the road, threatening dire consequences if they opened it, and hurried back to the village. The hedge-cutters were already on edge at having something witchy left in their care and nearly jumped out of their skins when Jack spoke to them from inside the sack. Having introduced himself, he said: 'If you let me out and help me to fill the sack with thorns instead, I'll give you some buttermilk.'

Despite their fear of the witch, the two men were happy to help. After a few minutes, the witch returned, picked up the sack and continued on her way to the cottage. The thorns poking through the cloth began to prick her.

'Jack, thee hast got some pins about thee, lad,' she grumbled. When she arrived at her cottage, she upturned the sack on to the kitchen

A witch in her kitchen feeding her pet devils or 'familiars'. Jack of Rempstone found himself in a witch's kitchen and only just escaped from ending up in her pot.

floor and then saw that she had been made a fool of. She was less than pleased. 'Jack, tomorrow I shall catch and boil thee,' she snarled.

The next morning, the witch called again and demanded buttermilk from Jack. Again he refused and again he found himself a prisoner in her sack. Walking home, the witch remembered she'd left some eggs back in Rempstone, so she left the sack with a road-mender and hurried back to the village to get them. Jack spoke up from the sack, promising the road-mender buttermilk if he'd let him out and help him to fill the sack with stones. When the witch collected her sack and headed for home this time, she heard the stones chink together and she muttered, 'Jack, thy bones do crack.' Back in her kitchen, she found she'd been cheated again. 'Jack, tomorrow I shall catch thee and boil thee,' she growled.

On the following morning, the adventure continued as before, but this time the witch did not risk stopping anywhere and went straight home. In her kitchen, she dumped the sack containing Jack on the floor and, after describing in deadly detail the ways she was going to chop him up and cook him, popped into her garden to collect some herbs for the pot. On this occasion, Jack had managed to arm himself with a knife and he cut himself free of the sack. Then he loaded it with all the witch's crockery and sneaked away.

When the witch returned, she got the pot boiling, dropped in some herbs and armed herself with a cleaver. Then she upended the sack. All her precious crockery fell out and smashed on the kitchen floor. The witch was beside herself with rage but decided that enough was enough. Jack's wiles were too much for her and she never begged at his cottage again.

THE BOY OF NOTTINGHAM

The most significant case of witchcraft in the county is the very strange one of the 'Boy of Nottingham'. William Somers, a teenager apprenticed to a musician in Nottingham, began to suffer from seizures, falling down as if dead, swallowing his tongue, weeping uncontrollably. The year was 1597 and conditions such as epilepsy or panic attacks were unknown. To his neighbours, it looked like a nasty case of possession by an evil spirit.

Things might have passed off without too much fuss, but well-meaning friends learned about a man with a reputation for exorcising demons and they called him in to help. John Darrell, from Mansfield, had travelled the country performing exorcisms and had become notorious for the trouble he caused rather than any help he might have brought. More than once he had earned the enmity of the established clergy. Ten years before, he had been involved in a case of possession in which the 'victim' admitted to faking her symptoms when the authorities became interested. There was a strong suspicion then that Darrell had engineered the hoax. It's clear he was no more than a conman of the Witchfinder General type, earning a living off the credulity and paranoia of the populace.

In *Witch-Hunting in England*, Andrew and David Pickering explain in some detail what happened when this dubious character arrived to 'exorcise' the afflicted 'Boy of Nottingham'. He declared that his first attempt at ridding Somers of his supposed demons had been successful, thus proving his worth. However, when the boy suffered another seizure, Darrell claimed that the evil spirits had returned. Somers was suffering, he said, for the sins of all the wickedness in Nottingham. He publicly declared that the city was a hot-bed of sin and depravity, and asked that all married couples refrain from physical intimacy to help improve the balance of purity in the place.

Having caught everyone's attention with this outrageous slur, Darrell then conducted a fire-and-brimstone sermon with young Somers as his star attraction. Somers obligingly acted out his symptoms for the congregation. Then things took an even darker turn. Darrell claimed that Somers's possession was the result of witchcraft, and named thirteen Nottingham women as responsible for the curse. In support of this charge, Somers would shriek or fall over whenever one of these women drew near to him (or he drew near to them). With Somers's help, John Darrell had now whipped up a state of hysteria in the town. As a contemporary commentator put it (quoted by the Pickerings):

'The pulpits rang of nothing but devils and witches; wherewith men, women, and children were so affrighted as many of them durst not stir in the night, nor so much as a servant go into his master's cellar about his business without company.'

Accusations of witchcraft now began to fly about and several people were in serious danger of finding themselves accused of the capital charge of witchcraft. If this situation had occurred a few decades later, at the height of the witch mania, it's doubtful that anyone would have listened to common sense. Fortunately, someone had the presence of mind to bring William Somers before the town council, accusing him of deception. Without Darrell to back him up, he soon broke down and admitted he'd faked all his symptoms. An inquiry was called.

John Darrell was too cunning a bird to let a small matter like an admission of fakery faze him. He declared that Somers was under the control of the Devil and his confession was a stalling tactic. Initially Somers went along with this and recanted his confession. The women accused of bewitching him were put on trial.

In court, however, Somers could not keep up his front and this time gave a much fuller admission of his wrongdoing. He now admitted to having faked all his fits and other signs of possession. He thought his employer would be so disturbed by these signs of witchcraft that he'd let Somers out of his apprenticeship, which he hated. He said that he had got the idea from reading accounts of recent witch trials.

Most damning of all, William Somers claimed that he had 'gleaned further tips from Darrell … that he might imitate them'. The trial collapsed and John Darrell found himself a prisoner instead. He was taken to Lambeth Palace to explain himself to the Archbishop of Canterbury and spent a year in gaol. Darrell never tried the same stunt again but remained impenitent, continuing to write and declaim against witchcraft on his release.

A woodcut showing a trial of witches in the late 16th century. The rough treatment suffered by those accused, even before being found guilty, is suggested by the man wielding a big stick over the cowering women. Those accused in the William Somers fiasco were indeed lucky that common sense intervened in time.

TWO TRAGIC WOMEN

Hundreds of years ago a murder was committed that almost immediately became part of legend. The tragedy took place in Clifton Grove, a pleasant wooded area by Clifton Village to the south of Nottingham. For many years it was a popular resort where the people of Nottingham would promenade during hot weather.

Little is known about the true history of the unfortunate 'Fair Maid of Clifton', as she became known. The story of her demise was set down as early as 1624, however. One later account states that she 'was debauched and murdered by her sweetheart' and 'was hurled down the precipice into her watery grave'. According to the same author, the spot became famous. It was pointed out to visitors and 'held in veneration by lovers'.

In 1803 the Nottingham poet Henry Kirke White published a poem based on the tradition of the Fair Maid which he called 'Clifton Grove'. In his poem, he gives the Fair Maid a name, Margaret, and presents her with a fate similar to the one described above, but with an added dash of the supernatural. Margaret gives her heart to a young man named Bateman, but the couple are soon parted when he is required to go abroad for a number of years. Nevertheless, she earnestly promises to be faithful to him while he's away and breaks a gold ring in two, one half of which she secretes in her bosom, giving the other to him as a token of her undying affection. Then White has Margaret make a rather rash pledge. She cries to Heaven:

> *'If, when he hail again his native shore,*
> *He finds his Margaret true to him no more,*
> *May fiends of hell, and every power of dread,*
> *Conjoin'd, then drag me from my perjur'd bed,*
> *And hurl me headlong down these awful steeps*
> *To find deserved death in yonder deeps!'*

Despite this earnest promise, after three years Margaret marries a wealthy man. Just six months later, poor Bateman returns and finds that she has betrayed his love. In despair, he throws himself into the River Trent and drowns. The remorseful Margaret is by this time with child by her husband. After the baby has been born, she creeps out of bed and, under cover of darkness, steals away into the night. She is never seen again but it is assumed she has suffered divine retribution for making her blasphemous pledge and has joined her lover in death. Indeed, local people would show the

The woods at Clifton Grove before the Great War.
The Fair Maid of Clifton came to a bad end here. (Picture the Past)

path 'down which the fair was borne, by the fell demons' to join Bateman in his watery grave.

Another, older version of the tale has the Fair Maid harried to her death by Bateman's vengeful spirit.

The true history of the Fair Maid of Clifton, if there was one, is now lost in the mists of time. Sadly, there is nothing fictional about the murder of Papplewick girl Elizabeth Sheppard. On the morning of 7 July 1817, Elizabeth left Papplewick and began to make her way to Mansfield, in order to find a job. She was just 17 years old.

The following morning some men on their way to work came across Elizabeth's body lying in a ditch. She had been brutally murdered, her head bashed almost to a pulp. It didn't take long to catch her killer. He turned out to be Charles Rotherham, from Sheffield. Rotherham appears to have been a vagrant, but one source describes him as a soldier, in which case he had presumably deserted his regiment.

On 25 July, Rotherham stayed in a pub in Redhill and there tried to sell an umbrella and a pair of girl's shoes. He found no takers. He left the shoes behind in his room but succeeded in selling the umbrella at Bunny, where he had wandered on to the following day. The connection between these items and the murdered girl were swiftly established and the hunt was on to track down Rotherham. He was found disconsolately leaning on a bridge over a stretch of canal between Redhill and Loughborough. He put up no resistance to the officers who apprehended him.

At the subsequent inquest, he readily admitted to murdering poor Elizabeth Sheppard but could give no reason for his action. He had never met the girl before; their meeting was a chance encounter. He needed money but that did not explain the savagery of his attack. He told the inquest that he had struck her repeatedly with a heavy hedge-stake before throwing her battered body in the ditch. This blunt and blood-stained instrument was produced as evidence 'and a thrill of horror ran through the spectators', according to a contemporary report. Unable to find any money on her, Rotherham tried to remove Elizabeth's gown, thinking he could sell it, but gave up and satisfied himself with her shoes and umbrella instead. He was hanged on Gallows Hill in Nottingham on 28 July.

The brutality of the killing and the tender age of its victim horrified the Nottinghamshire public. A monument was erected at the place where Elizabeth met her death so that the deed should not be forgotten. Its inscription reads: 'This stone is erected to the memory of ELIZABETH SHEPPARD of Papplewick who was murdered when passing this spot by CHARLES ROTHERHAM July 7th 1817 aged 17 years.' This can still be found beside the A60 Nottingham to Mansfield road, just north of its junction with the B6020, by Harlow Wood. It used to be a prominent feature on the highway but is now in a dip because of changes in the road.

Not long after the monument to Elizabeth was set up, rumours began to circulate that her ghost was haunting the spot. Coach drivers were particularly prone to seeing her, and they got to know her by the affectionate name of 'Bessie'. Over the years her memorial stone became known as the 'Bessie Stone'. According to Pat Mayfield, the murdered girl's apparition tended to manifest if anyone interfered with the stone. In 1956 it was struck by a car. A few nights later a young couple were strolling down the road when they were startled to see Bessie's ghost hovering over the monument. They described it as being 'of medium height with a long flowing robe'.

The stories of Bessie and the Fair Maid of Clifton lead us neatly on to consider a few of Nottinghamshire's legendarily haunted properties.

The Bessie Stone commemorates the murder of Elizabeth Sheppard and is said to be haunted by her ghost. (Picture the Past)

TWO HAUNTED ABBEYS

Newstead Abbey, near Newstead village, started life as an Augustinian monastery, founded by King Henry II as part of his penance for the murder of Thomas Becket. Like all such monastic houses, it was closed down by Henry VIII in the 16th century, after which it was converted into a private dwelling. Newstead Abbey then both grew and decayed, becoming a magnificent country house flanked by Gothic ruins. Today the house and grounds are open to the public and are in the care of Nottinghamshire Council.

Newstead Abbey was bought from Henry VIII by Sir John Byron in 1540. The Byrons continued to live here for centuries, their most famous son being the Sixth Lord Byron, the great romantic poet. This Lord Byron was also the last of the family to own Newstead. After backing the wrong horse in the Civil War, the Byrons lived as impoverished gentry for several generations, barely able to maintain the huge, rambling place. The poet loved Newstead's Gothic atmosphere and faded grandeur, and growing up there undoubtedly informed his verse. But he simply couldn't afford its upkeep and sold it to a friend in 1818.

Byron's father was not one of those who inherited Newstead. He missed out on that honour by running away with a countess, whom he later ditched for someone with a greater fortune. The Fifth Lord Byron was the poet's great-uncle, an even more colourful character (to put it politely) than either of his descendants. If the Sixth Lord was 'mad, bad and dangerous to know,' the Fifth was even worse: his bad behaviour earned him the sobriquet of 'Devil' Byron.

It was he who had left Newstead in such a ruinous state that the poet Byron had no choice but to sell it. According to one source: 'The noble woods that had surrounded it had been cut down and the stumps left; the lake was choked with mud and weeds, the house itself in a pitiful state of neglect and dilapidation. The damp came up from the floors, and the rain descended through the rotten roof, and the poet, coming into residence, was reduced to a small habitable corner, itself not altogether rain-proof.'

The house at Newstead Abbey as it appeared in the mid-1800s, after it had been thoroughly restored.

The new owner spent £100,000 — a phenomenal sum in those days — to restore the house and grounds to their former glory. So much money did he pour into it that he was unable to hold on to it himself for very long. There then followed a succession of short-lived owners and tenants. In 1916 both the owner of Newstead Abbey and its tenant died in the same week. Childlessness and unexpected deaths also dogged the history of the Byron family when they owned Newstead. Many saw this as a curse following the perceived sacrilege of converting a religious house into a private home. Even the poet Byron, on reviewing his troubled family history, felt compelled to write, 'it looks like fatality almost'.

In 1765 the Fifth Lord Byron was put on trial for killing a man named William Chaworth. Byron insisted that he and Chaworth had fought a duel and so got away with it, but many people continued to have their doubts about the incident. Despite his own brush with the law, 'Devil' Byron became incensed when his sister later got caught up in a scandal. He refused to talk to her again from that day forward. For years the poor woman followed him about, entreating: 'Oh, speak to me, my lord!' Her sad spirit is said to still wander Newstead Abbey, her plaintive cry of 'Oh, speak to me, my lord!' echoing in the passages after dark.

Newstead Abbey is claimed to be a very haunted place. One writer states that 'Devil' Byron haunts the house along with his unhappy sister and that they are seen to ride around the countryside in stormy weather. However, they do not ride together, showing that the enmity between them still holds. 'Devil' Byron hides himself away in a spectral coach, pursued by his ghostly sister on horseback.

According to his biographer Thomas Moore, the poet Byron was one of those who saw a ghost at Newstead Abbey. It was of a monk in a black habit. Known as the Black Friar, this apparition was supposed to have haunted the house since the Dissolution of the Monasteries. Many considered him to be a bad omen. His favourite haunts were the cloisters surviving from the medieval abbey and the room adjoining Byron's bedroom. Byron describes the ghost in *Don Juan*:

> '. . . *A monk arrayed*
> *In cowl, and beads, and dusky garb, appeared,*
> *Now in the moonlight, and now lapsed in shade,*
> *With steps that trod as heavy, yet unheard.*
> *His form you may trace, but not his face,*
> *'Tis shadowed by his cowl;*
> *But his eyes may be seen from the folds between,*
> *And they seem of a parted soul.'*

In contrast to the Black Friar, there is the White Lady. The author of *The Legend of Sleepy Hollow*, Washington Irving, noted that one of Byron's cousins saw this ghost. According to Irving, the young lady watched from her bed as the figure of a woman in white walked out of the solid room of her bedroom. It then swept across the room before vanishing into the opposite wall. Local tradition stated that the White Lady was the daughter of a relative of the Byrons who secretly married one of her father's dog-keepers and had a number of children by him.

The other ghost of Newstead Abbey is that of Sir John Byron, the man who bought it off the Crown and first made it into a home. His ghost is a rather distinctive figure, very short but with a great big beard. It has been seen sitting by a fireplace reading an ancient-looking book. Sir John's apparition also had a disconcerting habit one might have thought relegated to old horror movies: at midnight it would step down from his portrait hanging in the great hall before walking round the house.

The poet Lord Byron was the last of that name to live in Newstead Abbey. He is said to have once seen a ghost among the medieval ruins.

An amusing account of sleeping in the 'haunted chamber' beside Lord Byron's former bedroom was related by the American poet Joaquin Miller. He recalled:

'It was the loveliest night possible. The moon lay on the water like silver. Soon I undressed, and hastily blew out one of the candles, and set the other at the bedside, as I lay down. I did not dare to blow it out. It takes a great deal of courage to admit this ugly truth. The great, heavy and tattered curtains of yellow silk were like tinder, and it was a dangerous thing to leave the candle burning, especially after dinner. But it did not seem to me so dangerous just then, as to blow it out; and so, I think, I fell asleep.

'Suddenly I heard, or rather felt, the door slowly open. I looked straight ahead as I lay there, but did not move. A figure entered from the other door, but I could not see it. I felt it stop at the table. Then I felt it advancing on me where I lay. I distinctly heard the click of two candlesticks. Then I felt, or rather saw, that my light was being slowly and certainly withdrawn. I cautiously turned my head, and was just in time to see the patient footman, who had been waiting all the time outside, bearing away the lighted candle. Oh! How ashamed I was!'

A dramatic illustration of Newstead Abbey by Charles Harper, from his book, Haunted Houses, published in 1907.

Rufford Abbey is haunted by a mysterious monk and a White Lady.

Rufford Abbey is also said to be haunted. Like Newstead, it started life as a monastery but was later converted into a country house. Rufford was founded in the 12th century by the Cistercian order but was shut down during the reign of Henry VIII, who sold it to the Earl of Shrewsbury. The old Refectory was incorporated into the house, but the rest of the abbey was demolished. Much of the house suffered the same fate in the 20th century, knocked down when its upkeep became too onerous. Nevertheless, much of it survives and is a Grade I listed building, now in the care of English Heritage. It is situated in extensive grounds on the former abbey lands, part of which is a nature reserve.

According to a number of sources, Rufford Abbey is possessed of the ghost of a monk. In a black habit, he wanders the house and grounds and on one occasion was seen looming over the shoulder of a visitor as he was peering into a mirror. Two authors state that the 'face' beneath the hood is actually a skull. According to the Reader's Digest compendium of *Folklore, Myth and Legends of Britain*, there is an entry in the parish register for nearby Edwinstowe recording the death 'from fright from seeing the Rufford ghost'.

David Haslam, in his *Ghosts and Legends of Nottinghamshire*, states that the phantom monk is referred to as the Black Friar, adding that it 'seems to be of identical appearance to the Newstead ghost of the same name'. It is a curiosity that Cistercian monks wore white, not black habits. In his *Haunted Britain*, Antony Hippisley Coxe recalls being told about a black-habited monk who died in the house during a visit and that it is presumed to be his apparition that is seen. Mr Haslam ponders instead whether 'we have a travelling ghost in North Nottinghamshire, or is this an example of a recurring hallucination based on some fearful archetype from deep in the subconscious mind?'

Also in common with Newstead Abbey, Mr Haslam adds a White Lady to Rufford's roster of ghosts. She is thought to be Lady Arabella Stuart, who was born at Rufford in the 16th century. Later in life, Arabella found herself an unwanted presence, due to her bloodline, by both Elizabeth I and James I. She was held under house arrest in Hardwick Hall in Yorkshire for most of her twenties, but then enjoyed a renewed measure of freedom after Elizabeth's death. But Arabella became an unwitting pawn of political intrigue and ended up imprisoned in the Tower of London, where she died at the age of 30.

Another ghost reported from Rufford Abbey is of an old lady pushing a pram around the park. It's uncertain whether she has any connection to the distressing sound of a crying baby that used to disturb the residents' nights many years ago. There is a vague legend of a child who was chased through the house before being murdered, but who by, when, or for what reason has not been established.

THE TRIP TO JERUSALEM

A forthcoming book on the *Ghost Stories of Nottinghamshire* from Bradwell Books will go into much more detail about the county's haunted locations. One other iconic building does deserve to find its place in this book of legends, however.

The Trip to Jerusalem Inn (now prefixed with the over-used and redundant phrase, 'Ye Olde') is said to take its name from the days when Crusaders refreshed themselves here while en route to fight in the Holy Land. The current building is about three hundred years old but it stands on much earlier foundations. The pub is one of many claiming to be the oldest in England. It is situated at the foot of Castle Rock in Nottingham and is actually built into the sandstone, utilising existing caves for cellar space.

Before moving onto the strange tales connected with the inn itself, mention must be made of the legend connected with the cliff into which it is built. Castle Rock is riddled with caves. One of these is called Mortimer's Hole and is named after the Earl of March who successfully plotted with the 'She Wolf of France', Queen Isabella, to take the throne from King Edward II. After Edward's horrible death in Berkeley Castle, Gloucestershire, in 1327, Isabella and Mortimer effectively ruled the land, as regents to the 14-year-old heir. The young king, also called Edward, only put up with this arrangement for three years, however. Edward III had a very different character

*Ye Olde Trip to Jerusalem Inn in the heart of Nottingham
is one of the county's best-known haunted locations.*

to his weak and petulant father. At the tender age of 17, this determined youngster deftly staged a coup to get rid of the usurpers.

One night in 1330, while Mortimer and the queen were staying in Nottingham Castle, the young Edward and a small group of loyal soldiers crept into one of the caves in the rock and made their way up through a secret tunnel that had been created beyond it. In this way they were able to gain access to the castle unseen. Edward surprised the treacherous couple in bed and dragged Mortimer away, ignoring his mother's entreaties. Mortimer was taken to the Tower of London and later executed. Queen Isabella spent the rest of her life under house arrest in Norfolk.

Since this incident, the Earl of March's ghost is said to have haunted the cell in the castle where he was temporarily held. His pacing footsteps are claimed to have been heard going round and round on the flagstones. Mortimer's Hole, meanwhile, is supposedly haunted by Queen Isabella. Jennifer Westwood and Jacqueline Simpson, the authors of *The Lore of the Land*, believe Mortimer's Hole has been misidentified, however. They say the true tunnel was partly filled in many years ago and has only recently been rediscovered.

The Trip to Jerusalem Inn also has a reputation for ghosts. 'Foot-soldiers' have been seen walking through a wall, but it is not certain which period they belonged to. A phantom woman in crinoline appears on the stairs leading down to the cellar. Possibly she is the ghost of a 19th-century landlady. An indistinct male figure has also been glimpsed. The entrance to Mortimer's Hole has an eerie reputation and animals can apparently become agitated near it. A former landlady told David Haslam, author of *Ghosts and Legends of Nottinghamshire*, about another spooky place in the old pub, an area of the cellar popularly believed to have been 'a condemned cell' used by the castle above.

'As you walk in the cell, you know it's not right, you know it's evil,' she said. The landlady recalled that one night she was washing out some buckets at a sink near the so-called condemned cell when something 'like a grey mass' walked past her. She said: 'I had this feeling like an icy bar being passed through my body. It was a totally evil feeling, horrible. I wouldn't go down there for about three weeks. It really frightened me.'

Aside from its ghosts, Ye Olde Trip to Jerusalem also possesses several items with strange traditions belonging to them. There is a clock in the bar, for example, with something sinister about it. Dogs have been known to bark at it for no appreciable reason. Elsewhere there is an antique chair which women should be wary of using. It's claimed that any woman sitting in it will greatly increase their chance of becoming pregnant.

Finally, there is a legend about a cursed ship. Not a real one, obviously, but a model of a galleon. Together with numerous other seafaring artefacts, this little ship has had its home in the Rock Lounge for time immemorial. Its precise origin is unknown. The model is coated in thick dust and cobwebs because, so visitors are informed, no one is brave enough to clean it: at least three people 'died mysterious and unexpected deaths within twelve months of doing so'. For years the galleon was suspended from the ceiling, but so grotty did it become that it is now kept inside a glass case. Apparently, this was done because 'clumps of dust kept falling into people's pints'!

TWO HORROR STORIES

If the above stories have failed to spook you sufficiently, here are two more tales to finish with which might well make you shudder.

If you've ever wondered about the origin of the saying, 'To cut off your nose to spite your face', you'll find that the explanation is a most surprising and somewhat horrific one. As has previously been mentioned, during the Anglo-Saxon period Nottinghamshire was part of the Danelaw, the region of England under control of the Vikings. The conquering of northern and eastern England by Norsemen began centuries previously with a combination of peaceful settlement and brutal raids. A particular target of the latter were monastic houses, for their comparative isolation and the treasure they contained.

According to legend, in the 7th century a nunnery in Nottinghamshire fell victim to a Viking raid. This was Collingham, of which very little is known. For a long time it was thought to have been no more than a legend, and the following grotesque incident was therefore presumed to have occurred at Coldingham Abbey in Berkshire. However, in 1863 the foundations of an ancient building were accidentally uncovered in Collingham and recognised as belonging to the long-lost convent.

The story relates how the nuns at Collingham received word that a party of marauding Vikings was headed their way. They were almost upon them and there was no time to flee, indeed there was nowhere to flee to. Their fate was likely to be a nasty one. The abbess was concerned about one thing above all: that their chastity should not be compromised. To be killed was one thing, for to die in the Lord is no death at all. But to be deflowered, having wed themselves to Christ with a vow of chastity; this was not to be considered. If they could not flee and there was nowhere to hide, what could they do? The abbess decided that the only solution was to make themselves so physically unappealing to the marauders that they would be repulsed rather than attracted.

In a display of the most extraordinary commitment to her faith, the Abbess of Collingham took a razor and drew it down over her face, slicing off her nose and upper lip. Her horrified but dutiful sisters did the same, one by one. By the time the Norsemen arrived at the convent they found it inhabited by gruesome apparitions, sickening to look upon. Appalled, they wasted no time in slaying the brave nuns, who died comforted at least by the knowledge that their sacred vows had remained unbroken.

The ghastly story of the Collingham nuns may have some basis in fact, but we can be assured that the concluding horror story hasn't a grain of truth in it. The tale was told to folklore collector T.W. Thompson in 1914 by a gypsy named Reuben Gray. Mr Gray claimed that the adventure had happened to him. He explained that when he was a young man he had been strolling through Nottingham when he heard that a rich lady was advertising for a husband. She described her ideal spouse as someone young, dark and handsome and neither too short nor too tall. The young Mr Gray thought he would answer very well, so made enquiries as to how to find this unlikely woman. On asking around, a number of men warned him off making any further approaches.

'She's had seven husbands already,' they told him. 'And there's nobody knows what's become of 'em.'

Reuben Gray would not be daunted, however. At length he learned where he was to apply for the position of husband and did so. The advertiser turned out to be a perfectly charming and elegant lady and she seemed equally taken with the gypsy. They were married without delay. At midnight on their wedding night, however, Mr Gray awoke to find he was alone: his bride had vanished. Puzzled as to what had happened to the new Mrs Gray, Reuben vainly looked about for her but then fell back into a fitful sleep. When he awoke the following morning, he found his wife was quietly sleeping beside him.

Not used to married life, Mr Gray decided not to question his wife about her odd disappearance during the night. However, when exactly the same thing happened again the night following, he decided he ought to find out what was going on, albeit discreetly. So on the third night of their marriage, Mr Gray only pretended to sleep, and he felt Mrs Gray slipping ever so carefully out of bed. She then tip-toed out of the room. Equally quietly, Mr Gray followed her, and watched as she crept down the stairs. Mrs Gray left the house and flitted through the dark, her husband following at a cautious distance. Imagine his astonishment when he saw his pretty new bride's destination – the cemetery!

Mr Gray crept up to the cemetery's gates and peered in. His wife was kneeling on a freshly dug grave and scooping away the soft dirt with her hands. Then she sank down into the grave itself. His heart in his mouth, Mr Gray tip-toed over to find out what she was doing.

His wife appeared to be tucking into some sort of meal. Greatly puzzled, Mr Gray made his presence known.

'Hello, my dear, what are you a-eating on?' he asked.

'Corpse, you beggar, corpse!' she replied.

You can be sure Mr and Mrs Gray did not remain married a day longer.

The Abbess of Collingham prepares to disfigure herself: an extreme measure to stop pillaging Vikings from ravishing her.

ALSO FROM RICHARD HOLLAND FOR BRADWELL BOOKS

LEGENDS & FOLKLORE
Scottish
Wales
Wiltshire

GHOST STORIES
Cambridgeshire
Cheshire
Cotswolds
Cumbrian
Dorset
Essex
Hampshire & the Isle of Wight
Kent
Lancashire
London
Norfolk
North Wales
Oxfordshire
Scottish
Somerset
South Wales
Surrey
Sussex
Yorkshire

BY OTHER AUTHORS
Black Country & Birmingham
(Brendan Hawthorne)
Cornish (A Corn)
Derbyshire (Jill Armitage)
Leicestershire (David Bell)

London Underground (Jill
Armitage)
Staffordshire (David Bell)
Welsh Celebrity Ghost Stories
(South Wales Paranormal
Research)

FROM RICHARD HOLLAND
IN 2015/16

LEGENDS & FOLKLORE
Cambridgeshire
Hampshire
Dorset
Somerset

GHOST STORIES
Dorset
Herefordshire
Norfolk
Shropshire
Somerset
Warwickshire
Northumberland
Nottinghamshire
Devon
Lincolnshire

For more information visit
www.bradwellbooks.com